To:

From:

Published by Simple Truths, LLC
1952 McDowell Road
Naperville, Illinois 60563

Design: Lynn Harker, Simple Truths, Illinois

Photo credits: Getty Images, Masterfile, Corbis and Photolibrary

ISBN 978-1-60810-003-3
Printed and bound in the United States of America.

800-900-3427
www.simpletruths.com

07 WOZ 12

LAUGHTER IS AN INSTANT VACATION

Humorous Quotes On Life

Introduction

I love this book! Laughter is one of the **simple joys** of life. Therefore, I thought it made a lot of sense for Simple Truths to publish a book that's guaranteed to make you laugh. So I challenged some members of our team to look for their favorite **humorous quotes on life**. And I'm pleased to say they definitely rose to the occasion.

Laughter is to the soul what soap is to the body. It is sunshine in any life, and as our title indicates... **it is an "instant vacation!"**

So sit back and enjoy an unexpected getaway with a shot of inspiration!

Live with Passion,

Mac Anderson
Founder, Simple Truths

My sincere thanks to those individuals who contributed a lot of great quotes for ***Laughter Is An Instant Vacation:***

DEBBIE BASKIN

DARCI BERTONCELLO

JULIE DUMLER

DAN GREEN

LYNN HARKER

☼ KIRK HUMPHREY

TROY JOHNSON

TINA KALTENECKER

☼ JULIE KELLOGG

☼ BOB KELLY

BRYCE LOFCHIE

MICHELE LOFCHIE

JOELL LOUTSIS

SALLY REEVES

LANCE VANDERHAGEN

JOE VANEK

☼ KRISTI WHITFIELD

☼ KEVIN ZAHRTE

☼ *Denotes our Top 5 contributors!*

I was in a beauty contest once.
I not only came in last, I was hit in
the mouth by Miss Congeniality.

~ PHYLLIS DILLER ~

The best way to keep children home is to make the home a pleasant atmosphere … and let the air out of the tires.

~ Dorothy Parker ~

When you don't know what you're talking about, it's hard to know when you're finished.

~ TOMMY SMOTHERS ~

Camping is nature's way of promoting the motel business.

~ DAVE BARRY ~

So far on my 30-day diet,
I lost 18 days.

~ TERRY MCENTIRE ~

The trouble with eating Italian food is that five or six days later, you're hungry again.

~ George Miller ~

When I was kidnapped,
my parents snapped into action.
They rented out my room.

~ Woody Allen ~

I ask people why they have
deer heads on their walls. They always say,
"Because it's such a beautiful animal."
There you go.
I think my mother is attractive,
but I have photographs of her.

~ ELLEN DEGENERES ~

Adults are always asking little kids what they want to be when they grow up because they're looking for ideas.

~ PAULA POUNDSTONE ~

I buy expensive suits.
They just look cheap on me.

~ WARREN BUFFETT ~

I am not afraid of death, I just don't want to be there when it happens.

~ WOODY ALLEN ~

Politics is supposed to be the second oldest profession. I have come to realize that it bears a very close resemblance to the first.

~ RONALD REAGAN ~

A filing cabinet is a place where you can lose things systematically.

~ T.H. THOMPSON ~

I went to a bookstore and
asked the saleswoman,
"Where's the self-help section?"
She said if she told me,
it would defeat the purpose.

~ George Carlin ~

A word to the wise ain't necessary –
it's the stupid ones that need the advice.

~ BILL COSBY ~

If evolution really works,
how come mothers only
have two hands?

~ MILTON BERLE ~

He that falls in love with himself will have no rivals.

~ Ben Franklin ~

The nice thing about being a celebrity is that if you bore people, they think it's their fault.

~ Henry Kissinger ~

Never go to a doctor whose office plants have died.

~ Erma Bombeck ~

The best time to give advice to your children is while they're still young enough to believe you know what you're talking about.

~ Evan Esar ~

Guests, like fish, begin to smell after three days.

~ Ben Franklin ~

I am a marvelous housekeeper.
Every time I leave a man, I keep his house.

~ Zsa Zsa Gabor ~

Stress is when you wake up screaming and you realize you haven't fallen asleep yet.

~ Unknown ~

My brother was adopted.
Somebody left him on the back
doorstep when he was a baby.
We found him when he was 16.
We didn't use that door.

~ WENDY LIEBMAN ~

It is amazing how quickly
the kids learn to drive a car,
yet are unable to understand
the lawn mower, snowblower
and vacuum cleaner.

~ BEN BERGOR ~

Instead of getting married again,
I'm going to find a woman
I don't like and just
give her a house.

~ Rod Stewart ~

Those people who think they know everything are a great annoyance to those of us who do.

~ ISAAC ASIMOV ~

You can get by on charm for about 15 minutes. After that, you better know something.

~ H. JACKSON BROWN, JR. ~

Maybe I'm lucky to be going so slowly, because I may be going in the wrong direction.

~ Ashleigh Brilliant ~

After one look at this planet any visitor from outer space would say, "I WANT TO SEE THE MANAGER."

~ William S. Burroughs ~

I always wanted to be somebody, but now I realize I should have been more specific.

~ Lily Tomlin ~

They say such nice things about people at their funerals that it makes me sad to realize that I'm going to miss mine by just a few days.

~ GARRISON KEILLOR ~

Ekonomi
i nästan hela landet

It's amazing that the amount of news that happens in the world every day always just exactly fits the newspaper.

~ Jerry Seinfeld ~

A study of economics usually reveals that the best time to buy anything is last year.

~ Marty Allen ~

It's a dog eat dog world and
I'm wearing milk bone underwear.

~ NORM PETERSON (CHEERS) ~

The secret of staying young is to live honestly,
eat slowly, and lie about your age.

~ LUCILLE BALL ~

Insanity is hereditary.
You get it from your children.

~ Sam Levenson ~

The IRS has a special toll-free number for persons having problems figuring their tax forms. It's designed especially for those who like to listen to busy signals.

~ PAT WILLIAMS ~

Before I got married I had six theories about bringing up children; now I have six children and no theories.

~ JOHN WILMOT ~

If you look like your passport photo, you're too ill to travel.

~ WILL KOMMEN ~

I never forget a face,
but in your case,
I'll be glad to make an exception.

~ Groucho Marx ~

My favorite machine at the gym is the vending machine.

~ Caroline Rhea ~

If at first you don't succeed… so much for skydiving.

~ Henny Youngman ~

When I was a boy of fourteen, my father was so ignorant I could hardly stand to have the old man around. But when I got to be twenty-one, I was astonished at how much the old man had learned in seven years.

~ MARK TWAIN ~

The truth is
that parents are not
really interested in justice.
They just want quiet.

~ BILL COSBY ~

My wife has a slight impediment in her speech – every now and then she stops to breathe.

~ Jimmy Durante ~

I was so naive as a kid I used to sneak behind the barn and do nothing.

~ Johnny Carson ~

We hope that, when the insects take over the world, they will remember with gratitude how we took them along on all our picnics.

~ BILL VAUGHAN ~

Every day I get up and look through the Forbes list of the richest people in America. If I'm not there, I go to work.

~ Robert Orben ~

I belong to Bridegrooms Anonymous.
Whenever I feel like getting married,
they send over a lady in a housecoat
and hair curlers to burn
my toast for me.

~ DICK MARTIN~

Misers aren't fun to live with, but they make wonderful ancestors.

~ DAVID BRENNER ~

My favorite animal is steak.

~ FRAN LEBOWITZ ~

According to most studies,
people's number one fear is public speaking.
Number two is death. Death is number two!
Does that sound right?
That means to the average person,
if you go to a funeral,
you're better off in the casket
than doing the eulogy.

~ JERRY SEINFELD ~

My therapist told me the way to achieve
true inner peace is to finish what I start.
So far I've finished two bags of
M&Ms and a chocolate cake.
I feel better already.

~ DAVE BARRY ~

I plan on living forever. So far, so good.

~ UNKNOWN ~

I don't care to belong to any organization that accepts me as a member.

~ GROUCHO MARX ~

Last night I dreamed I ate
a ten-pound marshmallow.
When I woke up, my pillow was gone.

~ TOMMY COOPER ~

Only dull people are brilliant at breakfast.

~ Oscar Wilde ~

Never have more children than
you have car windows.

~ Erma Bombeck ~

I'm tired of all this nonsense about
beauty being only skin-deep.
That's deep enough.
What do you want –
an adorable pancreas?

~JEAN KERR~

My doctor is wonderful.
Once, when I couldn't afford an operation,
he touched up the x-rays.

~ Joey Bishop ~

I told my wife the truth.
I told her I was seeing a psychiatrist.
Then she told me the truth:
that she was seeing a psychiatrist,
two plumbers, and a bartender.

~ Rodney Dangerfield ~

I once shook hands with Pat Boone and my whole right side sobered up.

~ DEAN MARTIN ~

People who read the tabloids deserve to be lied to.

~ JERRY SEINFELD ~

I can resist everything except temptation.

~ Oscar Wilde ~

My one regret in life is
that I am not someone else.

~ Woody Allen ~

*I'm not going to vacuum 'til
Sears makes one you can ride on.*

~ Roseanne Barr ~

A Canadian psychologist is selling a video that teaches you how to test your dog's IQ. Here's how it works: if you spend $12.99 for the video, your dog is smarter than you.

~JAY LENO~

Everything is funny as long as
it's happening to someone else.

~ WILL ROGERS ~

You know you're getting old when you stoop to tie your shoes and wonder what else you can do while you're down there.

~ George Burns ~

To attract men, I wear a perfume called New Car Interior.

~ RITA RUDNER ~

I always arrive late at the office, but I make up for it by leaving early.

~ CHARLES LAMB ~

Cleaning your house while your kids are still growing is like shoveling the walk before it stops snowing.

~ PHYLLIS DILLER ~

Don't be humble ... you're not that great.

~ GOLDA MEIR ~

If you love something, set it free.
Unless it's chocolate.
Never release chocolate.

~ RENEE DUVALL~

The most important part of being a salesman is confidence. Confidence is like going after Moby Dick with a rowboat, a harpoon and a jar of tartar sauce.

~ ROBERT ORBEN ~

There's no such thing as fun for the whole family.

~ Jerry Seinfeld ~

The most remarkable thing about my mother is that for 30 years she served us nothing but leftovers. The original meal has never been found.

~ CALVIN TRILLIN ~

I'm at that age where if you flattened out all the wrinkles I'd be seven feet tall.

~ ROBERT ORBEN ~

The telephone is a good way to talk to people without having to buy them a drink.

~ FRAN LEBOWITZ ~

Life expectancy would grow by leaps and bounds if green vegetables smelled as good as bacon.

~ DOUG LARSON ~

I'm living so far beyond my income that we may almost be said to be living apart.

~ E.E. Cummings ~

I learned law so well, the day I graduated I sued the college, won the case, and got my tuition back.

~ Fred Allen ~

The first time I played the Masters, I was so nervous I drank a bottle of rum before I teed off. I shot the happiest 83 of my life.

~ CHI CHI RODRIGUEZ ~

I haven't spoken to my wife in years.
I didn't want to interrupt her.

~ Rodney Dangerfield ~

If you think something small can’t make a difference, try going to sleep with a mosquito in the room.

~ Unknown ~

When I was a boy the Dead Sea was only sick.

~ GEORGE BURNS ~

An archaeologist is the best husband a woman can have; the older she gets the more interested he is in her.

~ AGATHA CHRISTIE ~

Retirement at 65 is ridiculous.
When I was 65 I still had pimples.

~ GEORGE BURNS ~

Always go to other people's funerals, otherwise they won't come to yours.

~ YOGI BERRA ~

A lie can travel half way around the world while the truth is just putting on its shoes.

~ MARK TWAIN ~

The scientific theory I like best is
that the rings of Saturn are
composed entirely of lost
airline luggage.

~ MARK RUSSELL ~

The odds of going to the store for a loaf of bread and coming out with only a loaf of bread are three billion to one.

~ Erma Bombeck ~

My grandmother was a very tough woman. She buried three husbands and two of them were just napping.

~ RITA RUDNER ~

Walking isn't a lost art –
one must, by some means, get to the garage.

~ EVAN ESAR ~

I drink to make other people more interesting.

~ GEORGE JEAN NATHAN ~

I don't believe in the after life,
although I'm bringing a
change of underwear.

~ Woody Allen ~

Don't marry a man to reform him –
that's what reform schools are for.

~ MAE WEST ~

All you need is love.
But a little chocolate now
and then doesn't hurt.

~ CHARLES M. SCHULZ ~

I believe my wife is going to live forever. She has nothing but dresses she wouldn't be caught dead in.

~ BOB GODDARD ~

My husband wanted one of those
big-screen TV's for his birthday.
So I just moved his chair
closer to the one
we have already.

~ Wendy Liebman ~

I knew a man who gave up smoking,
drinking, sex, and rich food.
He was healthy right up to
the day he killed himself.

~ JOHNNY CARSON ~

My husband thinks that health food is anything he eats before the expiration date.

~ RITA RUDNER ~

I love deadlines.
I like the whooshing sound they make as they fly by.

~ DOUGLAS ADAMS ~

I spent a lot of money on booze,
women and fast cars.
The rest I just squandered.

~ GEORGE BEST ~

All you need to grow fine, vigorous grass is a crack in your sidewalk.

~ WILL ROGERS ~

I have an aunt who married so late in life that Medicare picked up 80 percent of the honeymoon.

~ DON REBER ~

Did you ever notice that the first piece of luggage on the carousel never belongs to anyone?

~ Erma Bombeck ~

If I'd known I was going to live this long, I'd have taken better care of myself.

~ Eubie Blake ~

I hate housework!
You make the beds, you do the dishes –
and six months later you have
to start all over again.

~JOAN RIVERS~

Keep your eyes wide open before marriage, half shut afterwards.

~ BEN FRANKLIN ~

One nice thing about egotists: they don't talk about other people.

~ GEORGE CARLIN ~

As parents, my wife and I
have one thing in common.
We're both afraid of children.

~ BILL COSBY ~

The most difficult years of marriage are those following the wedding.

~ Bethany Austin ~

My grandmother is over eighty and still doesn't need glasses. Drinks right out of the bottle.

~ Henny Youngman ~

Inside me there's a thin person struggling to get out, but I can usually sedate him with four or five cupcakes.

~ Bob Thaves ~

I like work;
it fascinates me.
I can sit and look at it for hours.

~ JEROME K. JEROME ~

Contax
Zeiss

Our children await Christmas presents like politicians getting in election returns: there's the Uncle Fred precinct and the Aunt Ruth district still to come in.

~ Marcelene Cox ~

When opportunity knocks, some people are in the backyard looking for four-leaf clovers.

~ POLISH PROVERBS ~

Housework can't kill you,
but why take a chance?

~ PHYLLIS DILLER ~

I used to think I was indecisive, but now I'm not so sure.

~ UNKNOWN ~

I cook with wine, sometimes
I even add it to the food.

~ W.C. FIELDS ~

*If you think nobody cares if you're alive,
try missing a couple of car payments.*

~ FLIP WILSON ~

I'm not offended by all the
dumb blonde jokes because
I know I'm not dumb...
And I also know that I'm not blonde.

~ DOLLY PARTON ~

All mothers have intuition.
The great ones have radar.

~ CATHY GUISEWITE ~

Never get married in the morning – you never know who you might meet that night.

~ Paul Hornung ~

If it weren't for electricity we'd all be watching television by candlelight.

~ GEORGE GOBOL ~

The trees in Siberia are miles apart, that is why the dogs are so fast.

~ BOB HOPE ~

The only time to eat diet food is while you're waiting for the steak to cook.

~ Julia Child ~

Don't worry about the world coming to an end today. It is already tomorrow in Australia.

~ CHARLES SCHULZ ~

A father is someone who carries pictures in his wallet where his money used to be.

~ UNKNOWN ~

Tell a man there are 300 billion stars in the universe and he'll believe you. Tell him a bench has wet paint on it and he'll have to touch it to be sure.

~ MURPHY'S LAW ~

Insanity doesn't run in my family.
It gallops.

~ CARY GRANT ~

Only two things are infinite, the universe and human stupidity, and I'm not sure about the former.

~ Albert Einstein ~

As a child my family's menu consisted of two choices: Take it or leave it.

~ BUDDY HACKETT ~

I've exercised with women so thin that buzzards followed them to their cars.

~ ERMA BOMBECK ~

Once, during prohibition,
I was forced to live for days on
nothing but food and water.

~ W.C. FIELDS ~

Adolescence is when children start trying to bring up their parents.

~ Richard Armour ~

I've been married so many times my certificate now reads: 'To Whom It May Concern.'

~ Mickey Rooney ~

It's good sportsmanship
to not pick up lost golf
balls while they
are still rolling.

~ MARK TWAIN ~

When I go to the beauty parlor,
I always use the emergency entrance.
Sometimes I just go for an estimate.

~ PHYLLIS DILLER ~

There must be something to acupuncture – after all, you never see any sick porcupines.

~ Bob Goddard ~

*Some cause happiness wherever they go;
others, whenever they go.*

~ OSCAR WILDE ~

If nobody knows the trouble you've seen,
you don't live in a small town.

~ UNKNOWN ~

I have enough money to last me the rest of my life — unless I buy something.

~ JACKIE MASON ~

There is nothing so annoying as to have two people go right on talking when you're interrupting.

~ MARK TWAIN ~

I've had bad luck with both my wives.
The first one left me and the second one didn't.

~ PATRICK MURRAY ~

If you hook up a politician to a lie detector machine,
the shrapnel could kill everyone in the room.

~ ARGUS HAMILTON ~

To keep your marriage brimming,
with love in the loving cup,
whenever you're wrong admit it;
whenever you're right shut up.

~ OGDEN NASH ~

I grew up with six brothers.
That's how I learned to dance –
– waiting for the bathroom.

~ BOB HOPE ~

Adolescence is perhaps nature's way of preparing parents to welcome the empty nest.

~ KAREN SAVAGE & PATRICIA ADAMS ~

I sometimes wonder if the manufacturers of foolproof items keep a fool or two on their payroll to test things.

~ Alan Coren ~

Laughter is the best medicine
for a long and happy life.
He who laughs — lasts!

~ WILFRED A. PETERSON ~